HURRICANES

THE WORST IN HISTORY

BY JENNA VALE

Gareth Stevens
PUBLISHING

Please visit our website, www.garethstevens.com. For a free color catalog of all our high-quality books, call toll free 1-800-542-2595 or fax 1-877-542-2596.

Library of Congress Cataloging-in-Publication Data

Names: Vale, Jenna, author.
Title: Hurricanes : the worst in history / Jenna Vale.
Description: New York : Gareth Stevens Publishing, [2025] | Series: World's worst disasters | Includes index.
Identifiers: LCCN 2024002711 | ISBN 9781482466706 (library binding) | ISBN 9781482466690 (paperback) | ISBN 9781482466713 (ebook)
Subjects: LCSH: Hurricanes–Juvenile literature.
Classification: LCC QC944.2 .V35 2025 | DDC 551.55/2–dc23/eng/20240229
LC record available at https://lccn.loc.gov/2024002711

First Edition

Published in 2025 by
Gareth Stevens Publishing
2544 Clinton St
Buffalo, NY 14224

Portions of this work were originally authored by Janey Levy and published as *World's Worst Hurricanes*. All new material in this edition is authored by Jenna Vale.

Designer: Claire Zimmermann
Editor: Megan Kellerman

Photo credits: Cover, p. 1 (main photo) Vikks/Shutterstock.com; series art (newsprint background) Here/Shutterstock.com; series art (fact box background) levan828/Shutterstock.com; series art (cover & caption box paper texture) Suti Stock Photo/Shutterstock.com; series art (hazard symbol) Maksym Drozd/Shutterstock.com;
p. 5 AB Forces News Collection/Alamy Stock Photo; p. 7 (upper and lower) NASA/flickr; p. 9 papa papong/Shutterstock.com; p. 11 ZUMA Press, Inc./Alamy Stock Photo; p. 13 Everett Collection/Shutterstock.com; p. 15 Sk Hasan Ali/Shutterstock.com;
p. 17 FEMA/Alamy Stock Photo; p. 19 Mark Pearson/Alamy Stock Photo; p. 21 (upper) Sky Cinema/Shutterstock.com; p. 21 (lower) MISHELLA/Shutterstock.com; p. 23 ymphotos/Shutterstock.com; p. 25 NASA Earth Observatory; p. 29 AMFPhotography/Shutterstock.com.

Printed in the United States of America

Some of the images in this book illustrate individuals who are models. The depictions do not imply actual situations or events.

CPSIA compliance information: Batch #CS25GS: For further information contact Gareth Stevens at 1-800-542-2595.

Find us on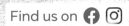

WORDS IN THE GLOSSARY APPEAR IN
BOLD THE FIRST TIME THEY ARE USED
IN THE TEXT.

A POWERFUL STORM

A hurricane is a big, powerful storm that can cause great **damage**. Hurricanes produce stronger wind and heavier rain than regular storms. They can cause flooding that destroys homes, farmland, and even whole towns. Hurricanes can hurt and kill people too.

Hurricanes happen all over the world every year. They usually happen during certain seasons, but not always. If the conditions are right, a hurricane can happen at any time. Each hurricane is different, and there may be different dangers from one hurricane to the next. Many hurricanes have changed people's lives in different ways throughout history.

HURRICANE MARIA CAUSED **DEVASTATING** DAMAGE IN PUERTO RICO, INCLUDING HUGE MUDSLIDES LIKE THE ONE SEEN HERE.

HURRICANE MARIA

IN SEPTEMBER 2017, HURRICANE MARIA HIT PUERTO RICO. THE STORM TORE ROOFS FROM BUILDINGS AND DESTROYED MUCH OF THE ISLAND'S POWER GRID. IT WAS THE DEADLIEST U.S. HURRICANE IN OVER 100 YEARS, KILLING AROUND 3,000 PEOPLE. MARIA CAUSED SO MUCH DAMAGE THAT EVEN AFTER MANY YEARS, PUERTO RICO WAS STILL REBUILDING.

HOW HURRICANES FORM

A hurricane begins when a storm forms over warm ocean water near Earth's **equator**. First, rain clouds appear. Then, wind spins around the center of the clouds. This spinning storm becomes a hurricane when the wind speed passes 74 miles (119 km) per hour.

The quiet center of a hurricane is called the eye. The heavy band of clouds around the eye is called the eyewall. This is where the storm's strongest winds and rain are. Hurricanes move away from the equator and may last from three days to two weeks. When a hurricane moves over colder ocean water or across land, it weakens and dies down.

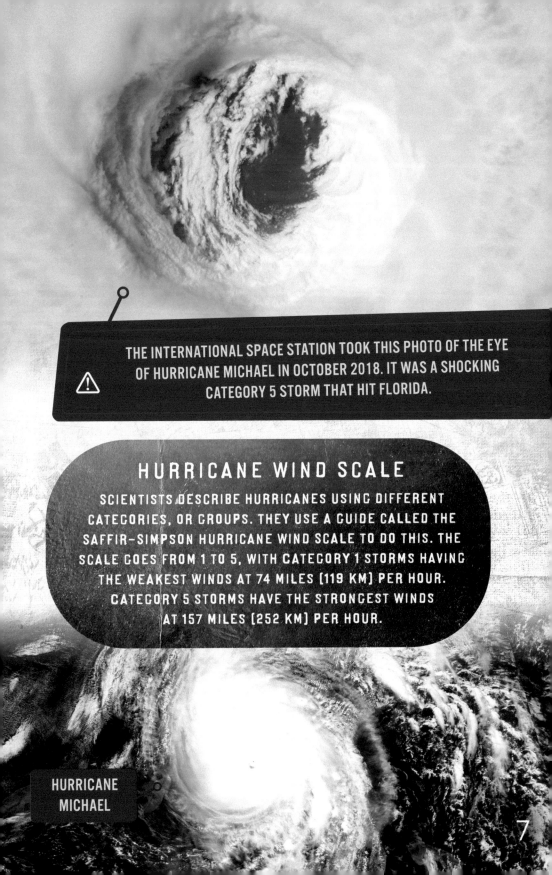

THE INTERNATIONAL SPACE STATION TOOK THIS PHOTO OF THE EYE OF HURRICANE MICHAEL IN OCTOBER 2018. IT WAS A SHOCKING CATEGORY 5 STORM THAT HIT FLORIDA.

HURRICANE WIND SCALE

SCIENTISTS DESCRIBE HURRICANES USING DIFFERENT CATEGORIES, OR GROUPS. THEY USE A GUIDE CALLED THE SAFFIR-SIMPSON HURRICANE WIND SCALE TO DO THIS. THE SCALE GOES FROM 1 TO 5, WITH CATEGORY 1 STORMS HAVING THE WEAKEST WINDS AT 74 MILES (119 KM) PER HOUR. CATEGORY 5 STORMS HAVE THE STRONGEST WINDS AT 157 MILES (252 KM) PER HOUR.

HURRICANE MICHAEL

BY MANY NAMES

The kind of storm we call a hurricane has different names around the world. If the storm forms over the North Atlantic Ocean or Northeast Pacific Ocean, it's called a hurricane. These storms over the Northwest Pacific Ocean are called typhoons. Over the South Pacific Ocean and Indian Ocean, they are called cyclones. The general name for all these storms is **tropical** cyclone.

There are about 85 hurricanes, typhoons, and cyclones every year. Most of them happen in the summer or early fall. Because they form over ocean waters, these storms affect coastal towns and cities more than inland communities.

TROPICAL CYCLONES
ACROSS THE WORLD

HURRICANES

North Atlantic
Ocean

CYCLONES

Indian Ocean

TYPHOONS

Pacific
Ocean

 HURRICANES

North Atlantic Ocean

CYCLONES

Indian Ocean

TYPHOONS

Pacific Ocean

⚠ THIS MAP SHOWS WHAT THESE STORMS ARE CALLED IN DIFFERENT PARTS OF THE WORLD. THE ARROWS SHOW HOW THE STORMS MOVE AWAY FROM THE EQUATOR.

FIRST NAME BASIS

SCIENTISTS GIVE EACH STORM ITS OWN NAME IN ADDITION TO THE LABEL OF HURRICANE, CYCLONE, OR TYPHOON. THEY DO THIS AS A WAY TO WARN PEOPLE THAT A STORM IS COMING. WHEN A STORM HAS A PERSON'S FIRST NAME, LIKE HURRICANE MICHAEL, FOR EXAMPLE, IT'S EASIER FOR PEOPLE TO KEEP TRACK OF THE STORM AND PREPARE FOR IT.

HURRICANE DAMAGE

A hurricane can cause damage in many ways. Wind blows heavy objects around and tears roofs off buildings. Heavy rain can cause floods and mudslides. The greatest danger from a hurricane, though, comes from storm surge. Storm surge happens when wind pushes ocean water far onto the land. People and animals can drown. Roads and buildings can be washed away.

Danger remains after the storm. Damaged buildings may be unsafe to stay in, and flooded roads are unsafe to drive on. People may need supplies, a place to stay, or medical help. If there's a lot of damage, rebuilding can take a long time.

THE GREATEST DANGER

WITH STORM SURGE, OCEAN WATER LEVELS CAN RISE 20 FEET (6 M) OR HIGHER ALONG THE COAST. IN ADDITION TO DAMAGING BUILDINGS AND ROADS, STORM SURGE CAN CAUSE DUNE **EROSION** ON THE BEACH AND POLLUTE FRESHWATER SUPPLIES. THIS CAN CAUSE EVEN MORE PROBLEMS FOR THE ENVIRONMENT AND PEOPLE'S HEALTH AFTER THE STORM.

⚠️ IN SEPTEMBER 2022, HURRICANE IAN CAUSED STORM SURGE IN NAPLES, FLORIDA, THAT REACHED 8 TO 12 FEET (2.4 TO 3.6 M) ABOVE GROUND LEVEL.

WORST IN U.S. HISTORY

In September 1900, a hurricane hit the city of Galveston, Texas. The U.S. government had **predicted** the storm would go up the eastern coast. Instead, it traveled across the Gulf of Mexico toward Galveston. Because the prediction was wrong, there was not enough time to warn everyone in the storm's path.

The wind speed was more than 130 miles (209 km) per hour when it reached land. The ocean rose about 15 feet (4.5 m) in just a few hours. The hurricane killed between 6,000 and 12,000 people, and it destroyed Galveston. It was the worst hurricane to hit the United States, and the deadliest natural **disaster** in U.S. history.

IN THIS PHOTO, A PERSON WALKS THROUGH SOME OF THE RUINS AFTER THE GALVESTON HURRICANE. THE STORM DESTROYED MORE THAN 2,600 HOMES AND DAMAGED THOUSANDS MORE.

IN THE GULF

SEVERAL FACTORS MADE THE HURRICANE MORE DAMAGING TO GALVESTON. FOR EXAMPLE, THE CITY IS ON AN ISLAND IN THE GULF OF MEXICO, WHERE THE HURRICANE BECAME A STRONG CATEGORY 4 STORM. ALSO, THE HIGHEST POINT IN THE CITY WAS ONLY 8.7 FEET (2.7 M) ABOVE SEA LEVEL, WHICH MADE THE 15 FOOT (4.5 M) HIGH STORM SURGE MORE DAMAGING.

GREAT BHOLA CYCLONE

The Bhola Cyclone of November 1970 was the deadliest cyclone in world history. It is also called the Great East Pakistan Cyclone. Scientists knew the storm was coming, but they had no way to warn people.

After the cyclone, East Pakistan became the country of Bangladesh. Bangladesh has always had terrible storms, but the 1970 storm was the worst. It struck at night when people were sleeping and caused storm surge that flooded one-fourth of the country. Between 300,000 and 500,000 people died. After the cyclone, Bangladesh created a program to warn people and better prepare for big storms. The program has helped keep more people safe in Bangladesh ever since.

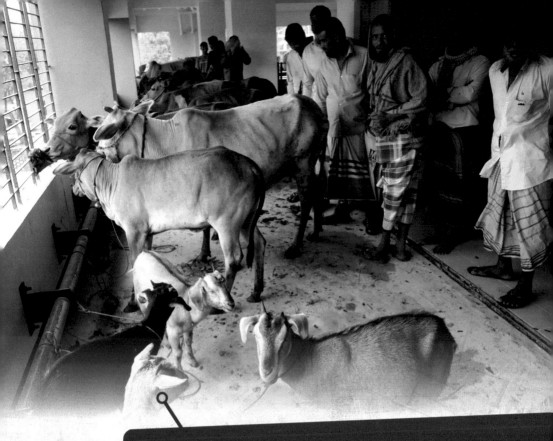

SINCE THE GREAT BHOLA CYCLONE, BANGLADESH HAS BUILT RAISED STORM SHELTERS ALONG ITS COAST. HERE, ONE OF THESE PROVIDES SAFETY FOR VILLAGERS AND THEIR LIVESTOCK DURING A 2023 STORM.

CYCLONE MARIAN

IN APRIL 1991, CYCLONE MARIAN STRUCK THE SOUTHEASTERN COAST OF BANGLADESH WITH INTENSE WINDS AND HIGH STORM SURGE. AROUND 140,000 PEOPLE DIED, AND AS MANY AS 13 MILLION PEOPLE WERE AFFECTED. STORM SHELTERS THAT HAD BEEN BUILT SINCE THE 1970 STORM SAVED SOME PEOPLE, BUT THE 1991 STORM SHOWED MORE WERE NEEDED. SINCE THEN, BANGLADESH HAS BUILT THOUSANDS MORE SHELTERS.

KATRINA IN NEW ORLEANS

In August 2005, Hurricane Katrina hit the southeastern United States. It was one of the largest and strongest storms to strike the country since the Galveston hurricane. It hit New Orleans, Louisiana, the hardest.

The rain, wind, and storm surge caused the **levees** in New Orleans to break. More than three-fourths of the city flooded. Hurricane Katrina killed 1,392 people. It forced more than 1 million people out of their homes. The damage was severe, and it took over a month for the floodwaters to **recede** or be pumped out. The cost of the damage was about $195 billion, making it the most expensive natural disaster in all of American history.

LEVEE FAILURE

NEW ORLEANS HAD A LEVEE SYSTEM AROUND THE CITY AT THE TIME OF HURRICANE KATRINA. HOWEVER, STORM SURGE UP TO 10 FEET (3 M) CAUSED MORE THAN 50 POINTS IN THE SYSTEM TO BREAK OR FAIL. SINCE THE STORM, THE GOVERNMENT HAS SPENT $14.5 BILLION IMPROVING THE LEVEES, FLOODGATES, AND DRAINAGE SYSTEM AROUND THE CITY.

THE LEVEE WALL SEEN HERE BROKE DURING HURRICANE KATRINA. IN SOME NEIGHBORHOODS, IT TOOK ONLY MINUTES FOR WATER LEVELS TO REACH PEOPLE'S ROOFTOPS.

CYCLONE
NARGIS

A storm called Cyclone Nargis hit the Southeast Asian country of Myanmar in May 2008. Normally, scientists would expect a cyclone in that area to move toward nearby Bangladesh. However, Nargis turned toward central Myanmar instead, where the land was the lowest in the country.

The cyclone's powerful winds blew storm surge up to 12 feet (3.7 m) over the land. The surge reached 25 miles (40 km) inland, devastating towns and villages. Around 2.4 million people were affected, and around 138,000 people died. Nargis was the deadliest cyclone of the 21st century so far, and the worst natural disaster in Myanmar's history.

⚠ THIS IS ONE OF THE MANY VILLAGES THAT FLOODED ALONG THE IRRAWADDY RIVER, MYANMAR'S LARGEST RIVER.

IN THE DELTA

THE AREA THAT SUFFERED THE MOST DAMAGE FROM CYCLONE NARGIS WAS THE IRRAWADDY DELTA. THIS AREA IS HOME TO MANY FISHERIES AND FARMS, INCLUDING 3.2 MILLION ACRES (1.3 MILLION HA) OF RICE FIELDS. MORE THAN HALF OF THE RICE FIELDS WERE DAMAGED. THE CYCLONE'S DAMAGE CAUSED FOOD SUPPLY SHORTAGES AND HURT LOCAL FARMERS AND MYANMAR AS A WHOLE.

19

SUPERSTORM SANDY

Hurricane Sandy moved over the Caribbean Sea in October 2012. It caused damage and dozens of deaths in countries including Haiti, Cuba, and Jamaica. Sandy then combined with other storm systems, becoming the biggest hurricane ever as it approached the United States.

Sandy became a superstorm, or an unusually large and powerful storm. It covered 900 miles (1,450 km) along the East Coast of the United States and affected 24 states. Millions of people lost power, and around 160 people died. Flooding was especially bad in New York and New Jersey. More than 100,000 homes were damaged or destroyed in New York City alone. Overall, the damage totaled around $86.5 billion.

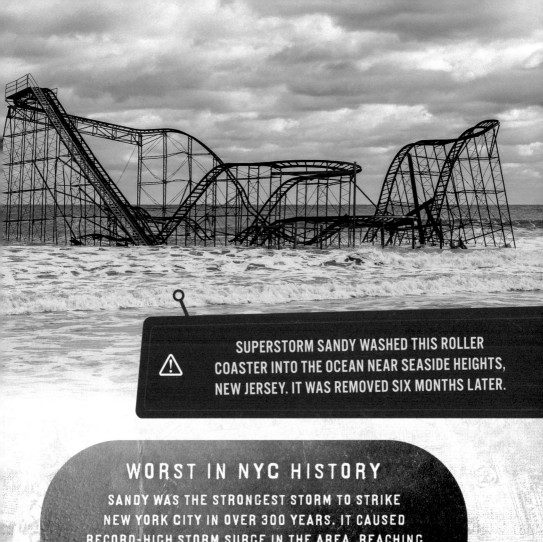

⚠ SUPERSTORM SANDY WASHED THIS ROLLER COASTER INTO THE OCEAN NEAR SEASIDE HEIGHTS, NEW JERSEY. IT WAS REMOVED SIX MONTHS LATER.

WORST IN NYC HISTORY

SANDY WAS THE STRONGEST STORM TO STRIKE NEW YORK CITY IN OVER 300 YEARS. IT CAUSED RECORD-HIGH STORM SURGE IN THE AREA, REACHING AROUND 14 FEET [4 M] HIGH. THE STORM SURGE SEVERELY FLOODED HOMES, ROADS, AND SUBWAY TUNNELS. IT WAS THE WORST FLOOD DISASTER OF THE NEW YORK SUBWAY SYSTEM IN HISTORY.

HOMES DESTROYED BY SUPERSTORM SANDY

SUPER TYPHOON HAIYAN

In November 2013, one of the worst typhoons ever struck several countries in Southeast Asia. It was a Category 5 storm called Super Typhoon Haiyan. It grew to more than 500 miles (800 km) in diameter. The eye of the storm alone was 9 miles (14.5 km) wide.

Haiyan hit the Philippines the hardest. The typhoon's winds reached a speed of 195 miles (314 km) per hour, some of the strongest of any storm in recorded history. The typhoon damaged or destroyed more than 1 million homes, and 4 million people became homeless. Around 6,300 people died. It was the worst natural disaster in the Philippines in more than a century.

⚠️ HAIYAN PUSHED THESE SHIPS ONSHORE IN THE CITY OF TACLOBAN IN THE PHILIPPINES. STORM SURGE WATERS REACHED RECORD HEIGHTS OF 24.6 FEET (7.5 M).

SUPER TYPHOON GONI

ANOTHER SUPER TYPHOON, GONI, STRUCK THE PHILIPPINES IN NOVEMBER 2020. WITH WINDS REACHING 195 MILES (314 KM) PER HOUR, GONI WAS AS STRONG AS HAIYAN. IT WAS THE STRONGEST STORM TO MAKE LANDFALL IN 2020. AT LEAST 20 PEOPLE DIED, AND MORE THAN 300,000 PEOPLE HAD TO LEAVE THEIR HOMES.

STORM
DANIEL

Hurricanes don't often form over the Mediterranean Sea, but in September 2023, a very strong one did. Storm Daniel first hit Bulgaria, Türkiye (formerly Turkey), and Greece. It then swept over Libya, causing floods that damaged many towns and villages.

The city of Derna, Libya, saw the most damage. Two of Derna's major dams burst, making the floods worse. About one-fourth of the city was destroyed. Around 40,000 people lost their homes, and at least 4,000 people died. Thousands of people also went missing. The damaged roads and floodwaters made it hard for rescue workers to bring help and supplies. It was the worst Mediterranean storm in modern history.

MEDITERRANEAN
SEA

LIBYA

EGYPT

⚠ STORM DANIEL, SEEN HERE, REACHED LIBYA IN SEPTEMBER 2023. MEDITERRANEAN HURRICANES USUALLY ONLY REACH CATEGORY 1 STATUS BECAUSE THEY FORM OVER A SMALLER AREA OF THE OCEAN.

MEDICANES

SCIENTISTS CALL A HURRICANE THAT FORMS OVER THE MEDITERRANEAN SEA A "MEDICANE," A MIX OF THE WORDS "MEDITERRANEAN" AND "HURRICANE." UNLIKE HURRICANES IN OTHER PARTS OF THE WORLD, A MEDICANE CAN FORM OVER COOLER OCEAN WATERS. SCIENTISTS HAVE FOUND THAT **CLIMATE CHANGE** IS INCREASING THE RAINFALL OF THESE STORMS, MAKING THEM MORE POWERFUL.

HURRICANE SAFETY

Scientists predict and track hurricanes in order to keep people safe. They use weather balloons, airplanes, and other tools to do this. If you live in a place where hurricanes happen, your family should plan what to do if a hurricane hits. Make sure you have enough food and water for several days. Check the local news on TV or online to know what is happening. Follow orders if you are told to **evacuate**.

Hurricanes happen every year. Some are stronger and more powerful than others. Many hurricanes throughout history have caused severe damage. Understanding more about hurricane dangers in your area will help you and your family stay safe.

BEFORE AND AFTER

BEFORE

Learn local news sources so you know where to look for information when a hurricane is coming.

Make sure your belongings are inside and your windows and doors are shut.

Check that any electronics you don't need are turned off and unplugged.

Make sure your disaster kit is ready and easy to find if you need to evacuate.

Make a plan with your family if you need to evacuate, and share the plan with other loved ones.

AFTER

Check local news for information about unsafe areas in your community.

With a parent, check around your home for any damage.

If the power went out, throw out any food that may have gone bad in the fridge.

Replace any items in your disaster kit that you may have used.

Check in with family and loved ones to make sure everyone is safe.

 HERE ARE SOME STEPS YOU CAN TAKE BEFORE AND AFTER A HURRICANE TO KEEP YOUR HOME AND FAMILY SAFE.

DISASTER KIT

THE BEST TIME TO PREPARE A DISASTER KIT IS BEFORE ANY STORM WARNING HAPPENS. AFTER A WARNING, MANY PEOPLE MAY TRY TO PREPARE FOR THE STORM AT THE SAME TIME. STORES MIGHT RUN OUT OF SUPPLIES OR NEED TO CLOSE BECAUSE OF THE STORM. BOTTLED WATER, FLASHLIGHTS, AND FIRST AID KITS ARE A GREAT START TO ANY DISASTER KIT.

FUTURE STORMS

Scientists have found that climate change may be adding to the power and frequency of some storms. It's linked to heavier rainfall too. For example, some scientists found climate change made the intense rainfall of Hurricane Harvey three times more likely. Harvey dropped about 40 inches (100 cm) of rain onto Houston, Texas, for three days in 2017. It was a devastating hurricane.

While hurricanes will always happen naturally, climate change is mainly caused by human activity. This means people have the power to slow climate change. Slowing climate change may decrease the dangers of future storms, flooding, and other **extreme** weather events, making the world safer for everyone, no matter where they live.

CLIMATE CHANGE IS ALSO TIED TO RISING SEA LEVELS. HIGHER SEA LEVELS INCREASE RAIN AND STORM SURGE, WORSENING FLOODS LIKE THOSE FROM HURRICANE HARVEY IN HOUSTON, SEEN HERE.

OTHER ENERGY SOURCES

THE MAIN CAUSE OF CLIMATE CHANGE IS BURNING OIL AND NATURAL GAS. USING THESE ENERGY SOURCES ADDS HEAT-TRAPPING GASES TO EARTH'S **ATMOSPHERE**, WARMING THE PLANET AND INCREASING CLIMATE CHANGE. SWITCHING TO OTHER ENERGY SOURCES THAT DON'T PRODUCE THESE GASES WILL HELP SLOW CLIMATE CHANGE. SOME OF THESE SOURCES ARE ALREADY USED TODAY, SUCH AS WIND AND SOLAR POWER.

GLOSSARY

atmosphere: The mixture of gases that surround a planet.

climate change: Long-term change in Earth's climate, caused mainly by human activities such as burning oil and natural gas.

damage: Harm. Also, to cause harm.

devastating: Causing widespread damage.

disaster: An event that causes much suffering or loss.

equator: An imaginary line around Earth that is the same distance from the North and South Poles.

erosion: The act of wearing away by water, wind, or ice.

evacuate: To withdraw from a place for protection.

extreme: Great or severe.

levees: Raised riverbanks used to stop a river from overflowing.

predict: To guess what would happen in the future based on facts or knowledge.

recede: Go down, become less.

tropical: Having to do with the warm parts of Earth near the equator.

FOR MORE INFORMATION

BOOKS

Cappucci, Matthew, and Hathaway, Stephanie. *Extreme Weather for Kids: Lessons and Activities All About Hurricanes, Tornadoes, Blizzards, and More!* Beverly, MA: Quarry Books, 2024.

Challoner, Jack. *Hurricane & Tornado.* New York, NY: DK Publishing, 2021.

Hopkinson, Deborah. *The Deadliest Hurricanes Then and Now.* New York, NY: Scholastic Focus, 2022.

WEBSITES

NASA Space Place
spaceplace.nasa.gov/hurricanes
Learn more about the science and tracking of hurricanes from NASA.

NOAA: For Kids
oceanservice.noaa.gov/kids
Learn more about climate and weather science with activities, videos, and more.

Ready Kids
ready.gov/kids/disaster-facts/hurricanes
Learn more about what to do before, during, and after a hurricane.

INDEX